THE STORY OF

HARLEY-
DAVIDSON®

JOHN PASSARO

ROSEDALE

SMART APPLE MEDIA MANKATO MINNESOTA

Published by Smart Apple Media
123 South Broad Street, Mankato, Minnesota 56001

Copyright © 2000 Smart Apple Media.
International copyrights reserved in all countries.
No part of this book may be reproduced in any form without written
permission from the publisher.

Produced by The Creative Spark, San Juan Capistrano, CA
   Editor: Elizabeth Sirimarco
   Designer: Mary Francis-DeMarois
   Art Direction: Robert Court
   Page Layout: Jo Maurine Wheeler

Photo credits: Corbis 4, 11; David M. Budd Photography 6, 16, 18, 23, 26,30,
32, 34, 35, 36, 37, 38; Corbis/Bettmann 7; Corbis/The Purcell Team 9; Corbis
/Dorling-Kindersley Limited, London 12, 20, 29; Archive Photos 13, 15; Fotos
International/Archive Photos 17; Corbis/Jerry Cooke 21; Corbis/Hulton
Deutsch Collection 25; Corbis/James Marshall 28; Reuters/Allen Frederickson
/Archive Photos 31; Courtesy of the Harley-Davidson Cafe 40, 41

Library of Congress Cataloging-in-Publication Data

Passaro, John, 1953–
      The story of Harley-Davidson / by John Passaro.
      p. cm. — (Spirit of success)
      Includes index.
      SUMMARY: Describes the origins and growth of the well-known motorcycle
manufacturer, Harley-Davidson, chronicling the company's successes and
failures over the past ninety years.
      ISBN 1-58340-003-6 (alk. paper)
      1. Harley-Davidson Motor Company—History—Juvenile literature.
2. Motorcycle industry—United States—History—Juvenile literature.
[1. Harley-Davidson Motor Company—History.] I. Title. II. Title: Harley-Davidson.
III. Series.
      HD9710.5.U54H3754 1999
      338.7'6292275'0973—dc21

                                                                              98-47571

9   8   7   6   5   4   3   2

Table of Contents

From Boneshaker
to Glide

The Harley-Davidson® motorcycle has become a symbol of American culture. To some people, it represents a **rebellious** spirit. To others, it represents personal freedom and a love for the open road. Most Harley® riders have a strong attachment to their bikes. Even people who don't ride may stop to admire what many believe to be the world's most beautiful motorcycle.

No one has ever fully explained the mysterious attraction of the Harley. It might be the roar of the engine. When 10 or 12 Harley riders travel together, the sound reaches thundering levels.

The attraction might be in the heavyweight size and the design of the machine itself. Harley-Davidson motorcycles feature shiny chrome **V-Twin engines,** polished teardrop gas tanks, darkly enameled paint jobs, and oversized speedometers. It was called a V-Twin because the motor consisted of two engine cylinders placed together in the form of the letter V. These **trademarks** of Harley-Davidson's traditional design haven't changed much over time. The company's popular motorcycles—from the Flathead™ of the 1930s to the Twin Cam 88™ introduced in 1998—have stormed across the United States for decades. Many years ago, Harleys became more than just a means of transportation. Today they are considered part of American history.

Every year thousands of motorcyclists cruise the highways to attend Harley rallies held in towns across the country. The riders swap stories, compare their motorcycles, and enjoy the Harley lifestyle. Some wear T-shirts that read "Born to Ride Free." Others wear black leather jackets with patches reading "Live to Ride, Ride to Live." The attachment is so strong that their bikes become a part of their identity—truly a part of who they are.

The motorcycle has fascinated the world's imagination for more than a century. A French engineer named Pierre

rebellious

Going against tradition or doing things differently than other people.

V-Twin engines

A motor that is typical of Harley-Davidson motorcycles, so called because it consists of two engine cylinders placed together in the form of the letter V.

trademarks

Symbols or names that belong legally and exclusively to one company. It may also refer to something that is unique about a company.

Michaux and his friend Louis-Guillaume Perreaux invented an early form of the motorcycle in 1868. Within 20 years, a German engineer named Gottlieb Daimler became the "Father of the Motorcycle" when he took a wooden bicycle and placed an engine between its wheels, which were also made of wood. At first, he was just testing a motorcar engine. In November of 1885, his son Paul was the first to

Since 1909, all Harley-Davidsons feature the famous V-Twin engine.

Walter Davidson poses with his motorcycle after winning a race in 1908.

ride the new bike. Paul Daimler managed to ride only a few miles. The bike became known as the Boneshaker because it was such a rough ride.

In the United States, the Harley-Davidson Motor Company started out gradually. In 1901, Bill Harley, age 21, and Arthur Davidson, age 20, were working for the Barth Manufacturing Company in Milwaukee, Wisconsin. They spent much of their free time tinkering with motorcycles. The boys said they wanted to "take the work out of bicycling" as they built their first motorized bicycle. It didn't work very well, but they kept trying.

logo
A graphic design
that symbolizes
a company. No
other company
(or individual) may
use another
company's logo.

The following year, Arthur's brother Walter, who was a machinist, joined them. His skill with machines made a difference, but he worked on the railroad and could help only part time. By 1903, the team managed to produce three motorcycles, built in a wooden shed that the Davidsons' father set up for them in his backyard. The Davidsons' Aunt Janet painted the gas tank a shiny black with pinstripes and even designed a **logo** for them.

Eventually, they hired one employee. In 1907, the third Davidson brother, William, joined forces with the team, and they officially **incorporated.** They called their new business the Harley-Davidson Motor Company and produced 150 motorcycles. By 1909, they had hired 35 employees, made more than 1,100 motorcycles, and moved into the first official company building on Juneau Avenue— the same site of the company headquarters today.

incorporate
To officially register
with the government
as a company.

The year 1909 was important to Harley-Davidson for another reason: The new company sold its first V-Twin engine motorcycle. The fastest motorcycle of its time, a Harley-Davidson could travel 60 miles (96 kilometers) per hour. The V-Twin engine has been a trademark design of Harley-Davidson ever since.

As time went on, Harley-Davidson had plenty of American competition. By the 1920s, more than 20 other companies designed and produced motorcycles in the United States, but Harley-Davidson was the world's largest manufacturer, with **dealerships** in 67 countries. In 1925, the company debuted the famous teardrop gas tank

dealerships
Retail stores that sell
motorcycles, cars, and
other consumer items.
Dealerships may
often sell only one
type of product, such
as Harley-Davidsons.

The V-Twin Engines: Through the Years

Since Harley-Davidson introduced its first V-Twin engine in 1909, it has periodically improved upon the original, producing faster, more powerful versions over the years to please its loyal customers. The following are the company's six trademark engines.

Flathead™	1930 – 1935
Knucklehead™	1936 – 1947
Panhead™	1948 – 1965
Shovelhead™	1966 – 1983
Evolution™	introduced in 1985
Twin Cam 88™	introduced in 1998

innovations

New ideas or ways
of doing things.

**Great
Depression**

The time during
the early 1930s
when the United
States and much of
the world suffered
from extremely
difficult economic
times with high
unemployment.

that would become a symbol of the Harley. In 1928, it introduced front-wheel brakes, improving the safety and handling of its motorcycles. Such **innovations** made Harley-Davidsons popular, but the biggest motorcycle of all—and some fans say the best—was that manufactured by its closest competitor, the Indian Motorcycle Company of Springfield, Massachusetts.

Then, from 1929 through most of the 1930s, the United States and much of the world fell into difficult economic times. It was the era of the **Great Depression.** During this period, thousands of businesses across the nation failed. No one had the money to buy luxury items, and that included motorcycles. Harley-Davidson sales dropped by more than 80 percent, and other manufacturers were hit even harder.

In 1936, Harley-Davidson introduced a new engine known as the Knucklehead™. Many believe it saved the company. Harley-Davidson was the first major American motorcycle manufacturer to build a big bike with a powerful overhead-valve engine that created speed and performance. By the end of the Depression, Harley-Davidson and Indian were the only motorcycle manufacturers to have survived the economic crisis.

When the United States entered World War II in 1941, the military recognized that the motorcycle provided a quick and inexpensive form of transportation. Harley-Davidson soon dedicated most of its production to making motorcycles for the American and Allied armed forces fighting in Europe and against Japan. Between 1941 and 1945, it sent nearly 90,000 motorcycles overseas for military use.

Many soldiers learned to love their Harleys during the war. Once they returned to the United States, they wanted to ride for sport. Harley-Davidson recognized their enthusiasm and introduced a new engine. The Panhead™, so called because it looked like an upside-down pan, appeared on the market in 1948.

During World War I, the American Red Cross used Harley-Davidson motorcycles to quickly reach wounded soldiers on the battlefield.

A 1942 Harley-Davidson motorcycle, manufactured for military use.

World War II helped Harley-Davidson recover, but the Indian Motorcycle Company continued to struggle after the Depression—as well as during and after the war. In 1953, Indian went out of business. Since then, for more than 40 years, Harley-Davidson has been the one and only motorcycle manufacturer in the United States. Although Walter Davidson died in 1942, and Bill Harley died only one year later, the company remained a family operation for many years. Arthur Davidson continued to play an important role in the company until his own death in 1950. Sons of the original partners took their own places in the company as well, including future company president, William H. Davidson.

In The Wild One, *actor Marlon Brando rode a Triumph, manufactured in Great Britain, but the film increased the popularity of all motorcycles—including the American-made Harley.*

civilian

Referring to a country's citizens, as opposed to its military.

Motorcycles reached new levels of popularity in the 1950s and 1960s. In 1954, a tough, young actor named Marlon Brando starred in a motion picture called *The Wild One*. The film gave American youth an image of a rebellious, outlaw lifestyle. Although Brando didn't ride a Harley in the movie, Harley-Davidson soon became the symbol of this lifestyle.

In *The Wild One*, Hollywood portrayed a life much like that lived by many World War II veterans. After returning from the war, some soldiers found it difficult to readjust to **civilian** life, so they restlessly roamed the country on their motorcycles. They traveled together in groups on their juiced-up army bikes. Motorcycling had become both a sport and a way of life. Recognizing the growing number of motorcycle enthusiasts, Harley-Davidson introduced the Sportster® model in 1957. The Sportster was a small, fast, and more affordable motorcycle. Today the Sportster continues to be popular, and it is the company's longest-running model. In 1958, it introduced the Duo Glide®, a motorcycle with special features that made the ride smoother.

A decade later, in 1969, Hollywood portrayed the motorcycle lifestyle again, this time in a movie called *Easy Rider*. In the movie, actor Peter Fonda's character rides what is probably the most famous motorcycle of all time: a powerful Harley named "Captain America," decorated with the American flag. His hog (a nickname for the big Harleys) sat low to the ground, and it had ape hangers—wide, flared handlebars that stuck way up in the air.

Young people of the day could relate to the movie. They were looking for change, and *Easy Rider* sent a message to the youth of the 1960s. It seemed to suggest that they could choose to live their lives differently than their parents had. Soon the freedom of the American motorcycle lifestyle captured the world's imagination. Fonda has said that when he traveled to Japan, young people (who hadn't even been born at the time he filmed *Easy Rider*) would come up to him shouting, "Captain America! Captain America!"

Dennis Hopper, Peter Fonda, and Jack Nicholson rode Harley-Davidsons in the well-known 1969 film, Easy Rider.

By the end of the 1960s, it seemed everyone wanted a big, powerful Harley. The company could not make enough motorcycles to meet the growing demand. Harley-Davidson found itself in a unique situation. It had the vast majority (up to 78 percent) of the business in a growing industry. It also had almost 100 percent of the heavyweight motorcycle market in the United States. (Heavyweights are the biggest motorcycles with the most powerful engines.) In 1961, it sold 10,000 motorcycles; by 1966, it sold three times that many—more than 30,000. Harley-Davidson was truly King of the Road.

To many Harley riders, the motorcycle represents freedom, fun, and independence.

Captain America

In the 1969 movie *Easy Rider,* Peter Fonda rode what may be the most famous motorcycle of all time: Captain America. It was an early-1950s Harley-Davidson, formerly used by the Los Angeles Police Department. The filmmakers actually used two of them, but only one survived the filming intact. It was stolen out of a warehouse and never recovered. The broken model was pieced back together and is now on display at the Harley-Davidson Cafe in Las Vegas, Nevada.

Hard Times Ahead

Despite the demand, and despite the remarkable loyalty of its customers, the Harley-Davidson® Motor Company arrived at the brink of death in the mid-1970s. How did it happen? Many motorcycle fans believe the company had two major problems. First, the company's **mismanagement** caused quality problems. Second, it failed to take seriously the aggressive competition from Japanese motorcycle companies.

In 1969, William H. Davidson, president of the company and the son of one of the original partners, urged **stockholders** to sell Harley-Davidson to another company, American Machine and Foundry (AMF). AMF manufactured a wide variety of sporting equipment, such as tennis rackets and bowling balls. The chairman of AMF, Rodney Gott, had been a "Harley freak," as he called himself, since World War II. Unfortunately, the company had no experience with motorcycles.

William H. Davidson felt that Harley-Davidson simply couldn't keep up with the demand for motorcycles. He believed Gott and AMF could help. He also wanted to protect the company from a **hostile takeover.** The stockholders agreed with him, and they sold Harley-Davidson to AMF for $22 million. After 60 successful years, the Harley and Davidson families were no longer involved in the management of the company.

In the 1970s, Harley-Davidson/AMF made several near-fatal mistakes. In order to meet the demand for its motorcycles, the company quickly doubled production—without concern for quality. It moved into an empty AMF factory in York, Pennsylvania, that was once used to manufacture bowling equipment. Since 1972, it has built only its engines at the original site in Milwaukee. It then ships them to York where the remaining components are manufactured and final assembly takes place.

With the new facility, Harley-Davidson was producing more than 60,000 motorcycles annually. Unfortunately, it

mismanagement

The act of running a business poorly or without care.

stockholders

Individuals who own stock, or shares of ownership, in a company.

hostile takeover

When one company takes over another by purchasing a large portion of its stock. A takeover is considered hostile if the company that was taken over does not want to lose control of its business.

executives

A company's leaders, such as its president and top managers. Executives make important decisions for a company.

made them so quickly that mistakes were bound to happen. Laborers used the wrong parts, old parts, broken parts—sometimes they even left out parts completely. Some engines leaked oil, and sometimes parts didn't work or even fell off a motorcycle during a ride. Not every bike was defective, but Harley-Davidson's reputation began to suffer.

In addition, some long-time Harley fans believed the company had begun to take its loyal customers for granted. Company **executives** assumed customers would put up with poor quality and keep buying Harleys anyway—just because they were made in America, and just because they were Harleys.

The company also underestimated its competition. Japanese motorcycle makers—including Honda, Yamaha,

Many motorcycle fans have credited the 1936 Knucklehead engine with saving the Harley-Davidson Motor Company during the Depression. Unfortunately, more hard times were to come.

A Harley-Davidson employee works on the construction of an engine in 1950. The company had long enjoyed a reputation for quality products, but during its years with AMF, Harley-Davidson nearly lost its positive image.

Kawasaki, and Suzuki—recognized that the American motorcycle market was the biggest in the world. For years, these companies had made lightweight motorcycles that sold successfully in the United States. Now the Japanese manufacturers took aim on the heavyweight motorcycles, and the unthinkable happened. Many riders abandoned the great American heavyweight manufacturer and purchased Japanese motorcycles. The Honda heavyweight, the Gold Wing, soon became the most popular bike in the United States. By the late 1970s, Americans were buying more Honda heavyweights than Harley-Davidsons.

Sales and quality continued to decline. AMF spent many millions of dollars on research to design and build new motorcycles and engines. What motorcyclists really wanted was the original Harley-Davidson quality. When Gott retired, AMF seemed to lose all interest in motorcycles. By 1980, Harley-Davidson's share of the American motorcycle market was only 30 percent, an all-time low.

AMF lost a lot of money because of poor sales. It tried to sell Harley-Davidson, but no other companies wanted it. Then a group of 13 AMF executives decided to buy the Harley-Davidson Motor Company. Vaughn Beals, the chairman of Harley-Davidson's board of directors, led the group. Although the company's value was more than $300 million, Beals and his team offered to put up only one million dollars of their own money, hoping to borrow about $80 million more from banks.

The banks agreed, and all the company executives took a ride on their Harleys to celebrate. They rode from York back to Milwaukee—the original home of Harley-Davidson.

The company encouraged the U.S. government to place high **tariffs** on Japanese motorcycles for the following five years. The government agreed, hoping to help an American company succeed. The tariffs meant that Japanese motorcycles were more expensive. This encouraged many

tariffs

The taxes charged by the government on imported products.

Americans to choose Harley-Davidson instead. In the meantime, the company had five years to regroup while the tariffs were in effect.

AMF's involvement came to an end, but it would be a long road back for Harley-Davidson. There were no guarantees it could survive. Sales continued to be poor. The company had to **lay off** 1,800 of its 4,000 employees.

Finally, in 1985, the banks who loaned the money to Harley-Davidson's leaders threatened to take their money back. Harley-Davidson didn't have the funds to pay back

lay off

To dismiss employees not because they do a poor job but because the company needs to save money.

Harley-Davidson frustrated its loyal customers during the AMF years. The quality of its motorcycles declined, and sales soon fell as well. At the turn of the 21st century, however, the company has regained its following. Harleys are more popular than ever.

both the banks and its **creditors,** and it came close to declaring **bankruptcy.** Under bankruptcy, Harley-Davidson would have had to close its manufacturing plants, and all company **assets** would have been sold. Employees would have lost their jobs. No more Harleys would have been made. Companies who supplied Harley-Davidson with parts would have lost their contracts. Then their employees would have lost their jobs as well.

Like many other American companies, Harley-Davidson faced tough competition from overseas. To have any chance of survival, Harley-Davidson needed to make some radical changes.

Harley-Davidson Sales: Through the Years

Number Sold

135,000

120,000

90,000

60,000

30,000

10,000

0

1903

1907

1909

1913

1920

1933

1936

1948

1953

1965

1975

1981

1988

1995

1997

Riding High on the Hog

Harley-Davidson® escaped bankruptcy. Richard Teerlink, the **chief executive officer (CEO)** at the time, convinced the banks to give Harley-Davidson a second chance. In 1987, the company admitted defeat at the hands of Japanese motorcycle manufacturers and began to study its competition.

From those studies, Harley-Davidson found three main keys to success that the Japanese had used, and then it set out to use them as well. First, it reduced the **inventory** of motorcycle parts kept in stock, waiting to be used. This saved money because the company did not pay for parts that would sit around for months, or even years, before they were used. Today Harley-Davidson only purchases the parts it will need in the near future.

Second, it began to measure the quality of every motorcycle through each step of the manufacturing process. It trained all employees to use new **quality-control methods** to ensure that Harley-Davidson produced only top-quality motorcycles. Third, it gave its factory employees the power to manage and make improvements in the manufacturing process.

In 1987, Harley-Davidson asked the U.S. government to end the tariffs on Japanese motorcycles one year earlier than planned. It had done so well that it no longer needed the extra help. President Ronald Reagan decided to visit Harley-Davidson headquarters in Milwaukee, bringing newspaper, radio, and television reporters with him. President Reagan proclaimed for the nation to hear that Harley-Davidson was "an American success story."

Harley-Davidson dedicated itself to restoring the strong connection it once had with its customers. In 1983, Harley-Davidson formed the Harley Owners Group (HOG). By 1998, more than 250,000 people had become members of HOG in more than 800 local groups worldwide.

William G. Davidson, William Davidson's grandson, is the vice president in charge of motorcycle design. In 1963, Willie G., as he is known, left the Ford Motor Company to help design Harley-Davidson motorcycles. He has dedicated his talent to the company ever since. Almost

chief executive officer (CEO)

The person responsible for managing a company and making decisions that help the company make a profit.

inventory

The amount of goods or materials kept on hand.

quality-control methods

Tests designed to make sure a product is well made.

every weekend, Willie G. rides his hog to rallies with other Harley® riders. Harley-Davidson executives, including Richard Teerlink, ride their bikes to motorcycle shows and rallies as well, hoping to learn what customers want. Harley-Davidson executives get mud on their boots and dirt on their leather jackets, while the competition usually attends such

Some Harley fans love their motorcycles so much, they do everything on them—even get married!

Today many motorcyclists collect and admire vintage motorcycles, such as the Harley-Davidson Panhead. It was built from 1948 through 1965.

shows in business-like suits driving luxury cars. Many of Harley-Davidson's employees like to spend their vacations touring the country, meeting with fellow Harley owners.

By reconsidering how it did business and dedicating itself to its customers, Harley-Davidson restored its reputation for high quality, winning back its share in a competitive marketplace. By the end of 1986, Harley-Davidson had taken back the top spot from Honda in the heavyweight market. By 1998, Harley-Davidson's share of the market was 56 percent. Once again, the demand for Harleys was much greater than the supply. The wait for a motorcycle could be anywhere from six to eighteen months.

Harley riders travel to different locations around the United States to attend rallies—large events dedicated to people who love Harley-Davidson motorcycles.

Rally Time

On June 12, 1993, Harley-Davidson enthusiasts from all over the country rode to Milwaukee, Wisconsin—the home of Harley-Davidson's headquarters—to celebrate the 90th anniversary of the first Harley ever produced. More than 100,000 motorcyclists joined the rally. 60,000 bikers formed a parade that stretched for 8 miles (13 kilometers). In 2003, Harley-Davidson will celebrate its 100th anniversary, and no one knows how many fans will flock to Milwaukee to congratulate the great American motorcycle manufacturer.

The Road Ahead

Recently the biggest problem for Harley-Davidson® has been finding a way to satisfy the huge demand for its motorcycles without repeating the mistakes it made in the past. In 2003, the year of its 100th anniversary, the company hopes to produce 200,000 motorcycles. To help achieve this goal, it opened a new production plant in Kansas City, Missouri. The new facility opened in 1998 and cost $85 million to build. It is used to produce the popular Sportster® model. When the plant opened,

Harley-Davidson expected to increase its overall production to 145,000 motorcycles, up from 135,000 in 1997. It would be the 13th straight year that production increased.

In addition to maintaining quality, Harley-Davidson must consider its newest customers if its success is to continue. Today's Harley® customer is likely to be a college graduate and a family man or woman (although more than 90 percent of Harley's customers are men). Its customers earn an average of almost $70,000 a year and sometimes may even own **stock** in the company. Nonetheless, it is still the rebellious, independent lifestyle Harley-Davidson motorcycles represent that attracts its customers.

Harley-Davidson has taken notice of these changes. Willie G. understands the importance of making improvements—the newest motorcycles, such as the Electra Glide® model, are equipped with luxuries such as stereo systems and cruise control. In July 1998, the company introduced its biggest and most powerful engine ever, the Twin Cam 88™. Only 18 of the 450 parts used in the new engine are carried over from the Evolution® engine. Like the Knucklehead™, Panhead™, Shovelhead™, and Evolution before it, the big Twin Cam 88 still stays true to the classic V-Twin shape.

Willie G. and the rest of the company are attempting to establish a relationship with the new customers without losing the original, **blue-collar** customers. Critics of Harley-Davidson, including many long-time Harley owners, say the company has priced the latest motorcycles too high for its

stock

Shared ownership in a company by many people who buy shares, or portions, of stock, hoping that the company will make a profit.

blue-collar

A term referring to working-class people or their interests. Historically, people who work in manufacturing and other laborers go to work in durable blue shirts.

The lure of the Harley attracts a wide variety of customers from many different backgrounds.
They all have one thing in common: a love for the great American motorcycle.

original customers to afford. They believe that Harley-Davidson now markets itself almost exclusively to wealthier customers. By 1998, the company priced the biggest motorcycles between $13,000 to nearly $20,000. Sometimes local dealers add thousands of dollars to the price because the bikes are so popular. Because so many people all over the world want to drive a Harley-Davidson, the company finally made an agreement with its U.S. dealers not to sell more than 30 percent of its total production overseas.

Harley-Davidson ran more than 2.5 million miles of road tests on the new Twin Cam 88, the latest V-Twin engine.

In recent years, the Harley-Davidson name and logo have appeared on many different products, including everything from clothing and children's toys to telephones and music boxes. Consumers can even buy perfume with the Harley-Davidson logo. Restaurants in New York City and Las Vegas use the name to attract customers. Some critics believe Harley-Davidson made a serious mistake when it

Every year during the first week of August, thousands of Harley riders travel to the town of Sturgis, South Dakota. They go there to admire other bikes, show off their own, and meet people who love their Harley-Davidsons.

Harley-Davidson's name now appears on a wide variety of products, from dolls to coffee mugs, mouse pads to beer mugs.

started using the logo on these products. In addition, Harley-Davidson requires that all new dealerships set up clean, modern stores—much different from the mechanic's shops where people once bought their motorcycles. As of 1998, there were more than 500 Harley-Davidson stores in 22 countries. Most of these locations sell not only motorcycles, but thousands of other items with the company name and logo as well.

The Harley-Davidson Motor Company has traveled through good times and bad since it produced its first motorcycle about 100 years ago. One thing is for sure: Harley-Davidson can survive no matter how rough the road may be.

Critics say that with such products, Harley-Davidson has begun to destroy its rebellious identity, turning away from its oldest and most loyal customers. Harley-Davidson executives respond by noting that the company sold almost $300 million worth of extra items in 1997, including about $100 million in clothes and collectibles.

The motorcycle industry, including Harley-Davidson, will probably experience ups and downs in the future, just as it has in the past. Motorcycles and Harleys may not remain fashionable forever, but Harley-Davidson plans to retain close ties with its loyal customers—both long-time riders and its newest fans.

As the company moves into its second century, it will continue to design exciting new products. Perhaps more important, designers of America's most popular heavy-weight motorcycle will make sure that some things never change. The teardrop gas tank, the V-Twin engine, and the famous Harley good looks are here to stay. The number one goal at the Harley-Davidson Motor Company is to continue its dedication to top-quality products. If it succeeds, the company will remain a lasting part of American culture.

The Harley-Davidson Cafe

In the 1990s, Harley-Davidson entered the restaurant business, opening the Harley-Davidson Cafe in New York City and later in Las Vegas, Nevada. The restaurants not only offer food, such as Road Burning Bar-B-Que and the Harley HOG Sandwich, but customers can take a quick tour through 100 years of motorcycle history as well. The New York cafe has one of the original 1903 Harley-Davidson motorcycles, while Las Vegas visitors may view the famous Captain America bike from *Easy Rider*. Even more impressive is the 28-foot-high, 15,000-pound (8.5-meter, 6,800-kilogram) replica of a Harley-Davidson Heritage Softail Classic bursting through the front of the Las Vegas cafe.

Harley enthusiasts can learn about the company with video and audio presentations. The cafes also feature the possessions of many famous Harley-Davidson fans—including rock stars, musicians, and sports heroes—who ride and love their Harleys. Customers may even take a virtual ride on a Harley, hoping on a vibrating motorcycle, revving the engine, watching smoke spew from the tailpipe, and imagining a ride on the open road.

Important Moments

1901
William Harley and Arthur Davidson attach an engine to a bicycle. Arthur's brothers, Walter and William, soon join them in their quest to create a motorized bike.

1903
Harley and the Davidsons produce three motorcycles.

1907
Harley-Davidson incorporates as a company.

1909
Harley-Davidson designs and manufactures its V-Twin engine, which will remain one of its trademarks.

1925
Harley-Davidson introduces the teardrop gas tank.

1929–1933
The Great Depression reduces production of Harley-Davidson motorcycles to 3,700—down from almost 30,000 a decade earlier.

1941–1945
The U.S. and the Allied Forces use about 90,000 Harley-Davidsons during World War II.

1963
Willie G. Davidson, grandson of William Davidson, leaves Ford Motor Company. Harley-Davidson Motor Company hires him to help design its motorcycles.

1969
Harley-Davidson merges with American Machine and Foundry Company (AMF).

1975
Harley-Davidson moves some of its production operations to a plant in York, Pennsylvania. Production reaches more than 75,000 motorcycles—twice that of recent years.

1981
On February 21, a group of 13 Harley-Davidson/AMF executives agree to buy Harley-Davidson back from AMF.

1983
To protect Harley-Davidson, the U.S. government establishes tariffs on its Japanese competitors.

1987
Harley-Davidson asks the U.S. government to end the tariffs on Japanese motorcycles.

1995
Harley-Davidson achieves record sales and produces more than 105,000 motorcycles.

1998
Harley-Davidson introduces the Twin Cam 88 engine after 2.5 million miles (4 million kilometers) of testing. The company opens a new plant in Missouri with plans to increase production of its popular motorcycles.

Glossary

assets
Money or objects of value that belong to a company or person.

bankruptcy
When a company (or an individual) cannot pay its debts, it may be forced to go out of business. It then pays creditors with any money that is left. This process is called bankruptcy.

blue-collar
A term referring to working-class people or their interests. Historically, people who work in manufacturing and other laborers go to work in durable blue shirts.

chief executive officer (CEO)
The person responsible for managing a company and making decisions that help the company make a profit.

civilian
Referring to a country's citizens, as opposed to its military.

creditors
Those to whom a company or individual owes money.

dealerships
Retail stores that sell motorcycles, cars, and other consumer items. Dealerships may often sell only one type of product, such as Harley-Davidsons.

executives
A company's leaders, such as its president and top managers. Executives make important decisions for a company.

Great Depression
The time during the early 1930s when the United States and much of the world suffered from extremely difficult economic times with high unemployment.

hostile takeover
When one company takes over another by purchasing a large portion of its stock. A takeover is considered hostile if the company that was taken over does not want to lose control of its business.

incorporate	To officially register with the government as a company.
innovations	New ideas or ways of doing things.
inventory	The amount of goods or materials kept on hand.
lay off	To dismiss employees not because they do a poor job, but because the company needs to save money.
logo	A graphic design that symbolizes a company. No other company (or individual) may use a company's logo.
mismanagement	The act of running a business poorly or without care.
quality-control methods	Tests designed to make sure a product is well made.
rebellious	Going against tradition or doing things differently than other people.
stock	Shared ownership in a company by many people who buy shares, or portions of stock, hoping that the company will make a profit.
stockholders	Individuals who own stock, or shares of ownership, in a company.
trademarks	Symbols or names that belong legally and exclusively to one company. It may also refer to something that is unique about a company.
V-Twin engines	A motor that is typical of Harley-Davidson motorcycles, so called because it consists of two engine cylinders placed together in the form of the letter V.

Index

Items in bold print indicate illustration.

Further Information

BOOKS:

Graham, Ian. *Motorcycles*. Danbury, CT: Franklin Watts, 1998.

Lord, Trevor and Peter Downs. *Amazing Bikes*. New York: Knopf, 1992.

Young Jesse. *Harley-Davidson Motorcycles*. Mankato, MN: Capstone Press,1998.

WEB SITES:

The official Harley-Davidson Web site: http://www.harley-davidson.com

Additional information:
http://www2.tower.org/museum/harley_davidson/harley_davidson.html

DATE DUE

Ant 3 Oct 14		
Joshua Ford		

DEMCO